Sabbath, Malcah Zeldis, American

Private Collection

KIDDUSH

OR

SABBATH SENTIMENT IN THE HOME

By HENRY BERKOWITZ, D.D.

Rabbi Congregation RODEPH SHALOM, Philadelphia, Pa.

Updated and revised by Rabbi Amy Schwartzman
and Herman J. Obermayer.

FALLS CHURCH, VA
5775–2015

ISBN 978-0-692-43023-1

First Edition 1898
Second Edition 1921
Third Edition 1966
Fourth Edition 2015
Prefaces to the Second and Third Editions are reprinted on
Pages 33 to 38

Picture Permissions

Sabbath by Malcah Zeldis, ©2014 Artists Rights Society (ARS), New York.

Jewish Sabbath from the collections of the African and Middle Eastern Division, Library of Congress, Washington, DC.

Friday Evening by Ben-Zion, Hirshhorn Museum and Sculpture Garden, Smithsonian Institution, 1966. Photography by Lee Stalsworth.

Sabbath and Havdalah Home Ceremonials, with cover for Hallah permission from Congregation Rodeph Shalom, Philadelphia, PA.

Mother Blessing the Sabbath Candles, with permission from POLIN Museum of the History of Polish Jews, Warsaw, Poland.

Rainbow Shabbat by Judy Chicago, with permission of artist. © Judy Chicago and Donald Woodman.
Photo © Donald Woodman.

Sabbath Hymnal, with permission from The Jewish Museum in Prague.

Illustration from Haggadah for Passover by Ben Shahn c. 1930. Art © Estate of Ben Shahn / Licensed by VAGA, New York, NY.

PREFACE

Sanctification of the Sabbath is Judaism's oldest rite. When Jews were little more than a band of nomads, long before they lived in houses, had formalized prayer services and wrote a syntactically structured language, they observed the Sabbath as a family ritual. The Torah's opening stanzas include, "After completing the work of creation God rested on the seventh day, and he blessed it." "Remember the Sabbath day to keep it holy" is specifically ordained in the Ten Commandments.

With the passage of time Sabbath rites have changed. And they will continue to do so. In the United States they have evolved in a uniquely American way. While Jews worship following their own historic tradition, they have adapted long established prayers to the majority culture. In 1898 Rabbi Henry Berkowitz, a Reform Jewish pioneer, authored *Sabbath Sentiment* to facilitate the consecration of the Sabbath in American Jewish homes.

For four generations Rabbi Berkowitz's small book has played a meaningful role in the Obermayer family's religious life. I recall fondly the portions that were read by my brother, sister and me at my parents' home in Philadelphia in the 1930's. My wife, Betty Nan (1932-2013) viewed *Sabbath Sentiment* as a necessary and joyful prelude to Friday evening dinners at our home in Arlington Virginia. In the 21st century I have participated in family services where my grandchildren recited from memory portions of *Sabbath Sentiment.*

Betty Nan was heir to venerable Reform Jewish traditions. (Her parents and both of her grandparents were married by Reform rabbis.) She in turn bequeathed that inheritance --- both modified and enhanced --- to the next generation. Her devotion to her religion was deep and abiding. She served as President of Temple Rodef Shalom of Falls Church, Virginia (1984-1985), and for over two decades played a major role in the congregation's leadership.

Because of Betty Nan's devotion to Reform Judaism and to *Sabbath Sentiment* it is appropriate that this lightly edited version be dedicated to her memory. She believed home Sabbath observance helped her to mold her own family into a cohesive unit whose members enjoy celebrating traditional festivals as a family.

It is the hope of Betty Nan L. Obermayer's family that *Sabbath Sentiment* will enhance the devotional experience of members of the Temple Rodef Shalom community --- a community of which she was proud to be a part.

   Herman J. Obermayer
   Arlington, VA
   2015-5775

"The Israelite people shall keep the Sabbath, observing the Sabbath throughout the generations as a covenant for all time: it shall be a sign for all time between Me and the people of Israel. For in six days the Lord made heaven and earth, and on the seventh day He ceased from work and was refreshed."

Exodus 31, v. 16–17

For many a Jewish person today, if one precious memory lingers it is often associated with a home Seder, a family together in religious joy. Why not enlarge the base of memory for our families and for ourselves by adding the beauty of holiness to the atmosphere of our homes on the Sabbath?

Thomas Mann, in his *Joseph* series, remarked that water properly channelled becomes a river, without the channel it becomes a raging flood. So it is with the human emotions. Without the bounds of ritual we would not know how much to sorrow, how much to rejoice.

Sabbath Menorah, *Ben Shahn, American*

SABBATH EVE SERVICE

KIDDUSH

KIDDUSH

Home Service For Sabbath Eve

The family table has a festive appearance using the best linens, silver, china, and flowers in season. A winecup and 'challah' (twistbread) are set at the head of the table. In the center of the table the Sabbath candlesticks are placed. The ceremony of ushering in the Sabbath is begun by the kindling of these candles by the woman of the house:

בָּרוּךְ אַתָּה יְהֹוָה אֱלֹהֵינוּ מֶלֶךְ הָעוֹלָם אֲשֶׁר קִדְּשָׁנוּ בְּמִצְוֹתָיו וְצִוָּנוּ לְהַדְלִיק נֵר שֶׁל־שַׁבָּת:

Baruch Atah Adonai, Eloheinu Melech haolam, asher kid'shanu b'mitz'votav, v'tzivanu l'had'lik neir shel Shabbat.

Blessed are You, Adonai our God, sovereign of the universe, who sanctifies us with Your Mitzvot and commands us to kindle the lights of Shabbat.

May our home be consecrated, O God, by the light of Thy countenance. May it shine upon us all in blessing, that these lights may be to us as the light of love and truth, the light of peace and good will. Amen.

SABBATH WELCOME

The leader of the household says:

Come, let us welcome the Sabbath in joy and peace!

Like a bride, radiant and joyous, comes the Sabbath. She brings blessings to our hearts. Workday thoughts and cares are put aside. The brightness of the Sabbath light shines forth to tell that the divine spirit of love abides within our home. In that light all our blessings are enriched, all our griefs and trials softened.

At this hour God's messenger of peace comes and turns the hearts of the parents to the children and the hearts of the children to the parents, strengthening the bonds of our devotion to that pure and lofty ideal of the home which is pictured in sacred writ.

Rainbow Shabbat (plate glass)
Judy Chicago, American

Responsive Reading

A woman of valour, who can find? for her price is far above rubies.

She looketh well to the ways of her household, and eateth not the bread of idleness.

She giveth food to her household, and a portion to her maidens.

She stretcheth out her hand to the poor; yea, she reacheth forth her hands to the needy.

She openeth her mouth with wisdom; and the law of kindness is on her tongue.

Strength and dignity are her clothing; and she laugheth at the time to come.

Her children rise up, and call her blessed; her husband also, and he praiseth her: "Many daughters have done valiantly, but thou excellest them all."

Grace is deceitful, and beauty is vain; but a woman that feareth the Lord, she shall be praised.

Give her of the fruit of her hands, and let her works praise her in the gates.

Proverbs 31, v. 10 ff.

THE BLESSING OF THE WINE

A wine cup is raised and the following is recited:

Let us praise God with this symbol of joy and thank Him for all the blessings of the week that is gone; for life, health and strength; for home, love and friendship; for the discipline of our trials and temptations; for the happiness of our success and prosperity. Thou hast ennobled us, O God, by the blessings of work and in love and grace sanctified us by the blessings of rest through the Commandment, 'Six days shalt thou labor and do all thy work, but the seventh day is the Sabbath hallowed unto the Lord thy God.'

Jewish Sabbath, *Amsterdam, Holland, 1713*

THE BENEDICTIONS

בָּרוּךְ אַתָּה יְהֹוָה אֱלֹהֵינוּ מֶלֶךְ הָעוֹלָם
בּוֹרֵא פְּרִי הַגָּפֶן:

Baruch Atah Adonai, Eloheinu Melech haolam, borei p'ri hagafen.

We praise You, Adonai our God, Sovereign of the universe, Creator of the fruit of the vine.

The goblet is passed as a loving cup and each in turn drinks therefrom.

THE BLESSING OF THE BREAD

After breaking off a piece of challah and dipping it in salt, a member of the family says:

בָּרוּךְ אַתָּה יְהֹוָה אֱלֹהֵינוּ מֶלֶךְ הָעוֹלָם
הַמּוֹצִיא לֶחֶם מִן־הָאָרֶץ:

Baruch Atah Adonai, Eloheinu Melech haolam, hamotzi lechem min ha'aretz.

We praise You, Adonai our God, Sovereign of the universe, who brings forth bread from the earth.

Each one at the table likewise partakes of the bread and salt.

Mother Blessing the Sabbath Candles, *Mayer Kirschenblatt, Polish*

Museum of the History of Polish Jews, Warsaw, Poland

BLESSING THE CHILDREN

The parent with hands upon the head of each child in turn silently pronounces such a blessing as the heart may prompt, or uses one of the following benedictions:

For sons:

יְשִׂימְךָ אֱלֹהִים כְּאֶפְרַיִם וְכִמְנַשֶּׁה:

Y'simcha Elohim k'Efrayim v'chiM'nasheh.

For daughters:

יְשִׂימֵךְ אֱלֹהִים כְּשָׂרָה רִבְקָה רָחֵל וְלֵאָה:

Y'simeich Elohim k'Sarah, Rivkah, Rachel, v'Leah.

May God bless you and guard you.

May God's light shine upon you, and may God be gracious to you.

May God's presence be with you and give you peace.

The Sabbath meal is served.

Sabbath Hymnal, Prague, Czech Republic, 1514

Jewish Museum in Prague, Czech Republic

GRACE AFTER THE MEAL

O Lord, Thou art our shepherd, and we shall not want. Thou openest Thy hand and satisfiest the needs of every living being. We thank Thee for the gifts of Thy bounty which we have enjoyed at this table. As Thou hast provided for us hitherto, so mayest Thou sustain us throughout our lives. Thy kindness endureth forever, and we put our trust in Thee.

While we enjoy Thy gifts, may we never forget the needy, nor allow those who want, to be forsaken. May our table be an altar of lovingkindness, and our home a temple in which Thy spirit of goodness dwells.

בָּרוּךְ אַתָּה יְהוָה הַזָּן אֶת־הַכֹּל׃

Baruch Atah Adonai, hazan et hakol.

We praise You, O God, Source of food for all who live. AMEN.

Sabbath Home Ceremonials
1. Sabbath Candlesticks; 2. Hallah Knife; 3. Kiddush Cup; 4. Kiddush Plate

Obermayer Collection, Congregation Rodeph Shalom, Philadelphia, PA

Whenever possible the members of the family should now go together to the synagogue or temple and join in public worship, sharing the mood and inspiration of the Sabbath with the larger community.

At other times the family may join in songs, much as is done at the Passover Seder.

Obermayer Collection, Congregation Rodeph Shalom, Philadelphia, PA

L'CHO DODI

How good it is to thank the Lord,
>To praise Thy name, O Thou most high;
To tell Thy kindness through the day,
>Thy faithfulness when night draws nigh.

With joyous psalms and with the harp,
>Will I Thy marvels gladly sing;
Thy works have made my heart rejoice;
>I triumph in Thy work, my King!

Like stately palm the righteous thrive,
>As cedar fair they flourish free
In God's own house; His courts alone
>Their dwelling place and home shall be.

Still, in old age, ripe fruit they bear,
>Verdant and fresh they still remain
To prove that God, my rock of help,
>His righteousness doth e'er maintain.

SABBATH NIGHT SERVICE
HAVDALAH

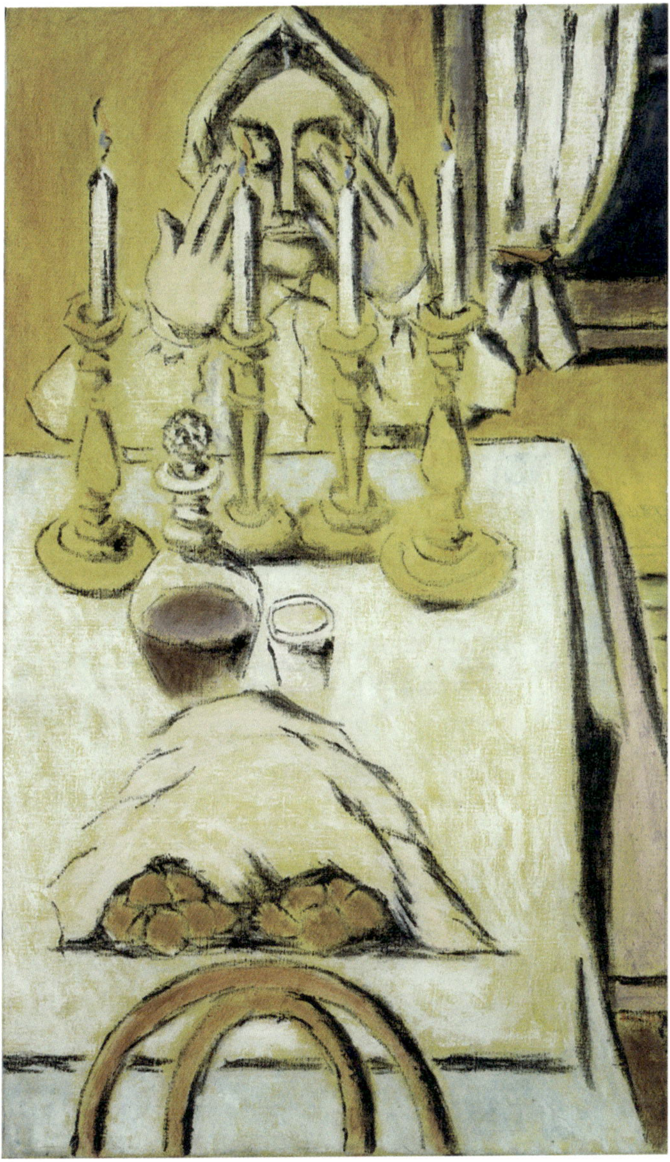

Hirshhorn Museum, Washington, DC

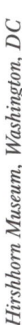

Friday Evening, *Ben-Zion, American*

HAVDALAH

As the incoming of the Sabbath was marked by the act of Sanctification or Kiddush so the outgoing of the Sabbath was characterized by an observance called Havdalah or "Separation." We discover in this ceremonial a singularly beautiful and inspiring purpose. I find this not so much in the sentiment of regret that Sabbath rest and Sabbath joy are ended (which is the usual interpretation) as in the impulse these have given to dedicate and restore our energies to the work of another week.

"Six days shalt thou labor" is to be recognized as a divine blessing, no less than is "Observe the Sabbath rest." The honor, the dignity, the joy of our labor is therefore to be consecrated also with the blessing of the symbol of joy, the "Wine Cup." "Wine that maketh glad the heart of man and bread that strengthens the heart of man,"–sang the Psalmist.

The choicest of all of nature's gifts are the fragrant spices. Emblems and tokens are they of all nature's products. The artistic spice box is uplifted and the delightful aroma inhaled. The spirit thus exalted breathes forth its grateful sentiment in words of benediction.

The rabbinical legend sets forth that "Fire was one of the things God had left uncreated when Sabbath set in; but after the close of the Sabbath God endowed man with reason which prompted him to take two stones and grind them together till the sparks leaped forth whereupon he broke forth in praise and recited the blessing for fire and light."

With this divine power at his command he applied his faculties to the labor awaiting him and so became co-worker with God the Creator of the World.

Tasting the wine, smelling the spices, seeing the radiance, hearing the melody of song and feeling the objects, bring into play the five senses as the tools for our work.

Havdalah Home Ceremonials
1. Kiddush Cup; 2. Spice Box; 3. Havdalah Candle; 4. Havdalah Plate

Plate Translation
Good Week-Good Year
"The Commandment of The Lord is pure, enlightening the eyes."

HAVDALAH SERVICE

(The leader lights the Havdalah Candle saying the following blessing:)

בָּרוּךְ אַתָּה יְהֹוָה אֱלֹהֵינוּ מֶלֶךְ הָעוֹלָם
בּוֹרֵא מְאוֹרֵי הָאֵשׁ:

Baruch Atah Adonai, Eloheinu Melech haolam, borei m'orei haeish.

We praise You, Adonai our God, Sovereign of the universe, Creator of the lights of fire.

Last night we began the Sabbath with the lighting of the Sabbath Candle. Tonight we end the Sabbath with the lighting of the Havdalah Candle. Havdalah means separation. This Service teaches us that we must differentiate between the holy and the profane, between what is right and what is wrong, between what is true and what is false. Man alone of all the animals in the world can make this choice. But to choose correctly we must have knowledge, courage and concern. The Sabbath in our tradition is a day devoted to the strengthening of our moral judgment by heightening our religious sensitivity, broadening our knowledge of truth and righteousness, and deepening our love for God and our fellow man. Now at the end of the Sabbath Day we must carry whatever inspiration, learning, and dedication we have received from the Sabbath into the rest of the week.

THE WINE CUP

(Leader lifts cup of wine and asks everyone to join in the blessing.)

בָּרוּךְ אַתָּה יְהוָֹה אֱלֹהֵינוּ מֶלֶךְ הָעוֹלָם
בּוֹרֵא פְּרִי הַגָּפֶן:

Baruch Atah Adonai, Eloheinu Melech haolam, borei p'ri hagafen.

We praise You, Adonai our God, Sovereign of the universe, who creates the fruit of the vine.

As we began the Sabbath with the Blessing of the Wine, so, too, do we end it. Judaism teaches that nothing is intrinsically holy or profane, good or evil. It all depends on what we do, how we do it, and why we do it. Some people prohibit wine because it may make of man a fool or a drunkard. But the rabbis sanctified wine by using it in each Service to bless our holidays and our feasts, and so to elevate our use of wine. Havdalah teaches us that though we must separate the holy, the true, and the good from their opposites, we must not abandon the latter. Everything that is wrong may be corrected, everything that is profane may be sanctified. Everything is capable of redemption, everyone is capable of repentance.

THE SPICE BOX

(The leader now lifts the spice box, shakes it, and smells it after all have joined in the blessings.)

בָּרוּךְ אַתָּה יְהֹוָה אֱלֹהֵינוּ מֶלֶךְ הָעוֹלָם
בּוֹרֵא מִינֵי בְשָׂמִים:

Baruch Atah Adonai, Eloheinu Melech haolam, borei minei v'samim.

We praise You, Adonai our God, Sovereign of the universe, who creates varieties of fragrant spices.

(As Spice Box is passed from hand to hand, the leader begins the singing of Shovua Tov.)

Shovua Tov, Shovua Tov,
Shovua Tov, Shovua Tov,

> A good week, a week of peace,
> May gladness reign and joy increase.

Shovua Tov, Shovua Tov,
Shovua Tov, Shovua Tov.

BENEDICTION

Blessed art Thou, O Lord our God, ruler of the universe, who hast made a separation between light and darkness; between Sabbath and work days; between right and wrong; between sacred and profane. O help us to serve Thee as we consecrate ourselves anew to the labor Thou hast ordained for each one of us to do. AMEN!

PREFACE TO SECOND EDITION

A number of parents and friends were gathered in absorbed interest about a group of bright young children to whom an enthusiastic teacher was giving a lesson on the Sabbath, with the beautiful and instructive symbolism of the Kiddush, or service for the Sanctification of the Sabbath eve in the home. An animated discussion ensued. It was at the second Assembly convened by the Jewish Chautauqua Society. There was much enthusiasm. Earnest expression was given to the need, felt to be general, for some practical handbook to serve young parents introducing or restoring to their homes religious observances in a form that would make a genuine and vital appeal. Thus the writer was urged to prepare and publish this little book in 1898. It was accorded a generous welcome.

The schools had come to a true evaluation of symbolic teaching and object lessons. Intelligent Jewish parents apprehended that this discovery of the "New Education" was in fact only a restatement of an old principle of the old Jewish teachers who had founded it on the Biblical injunction, "When in days to come thy son shall ask thee then shalt thou say, etc." Thus there had been evolved those festivals, institutes, rites and ceremonies which, through centuries, have touched the minds and quickened the hearts of Jewish children. Why not then reclaim these precious treasures—products of the Jewish genius!

They had fallen into disuse because of the general revolt against all formalism, and formalism in religion was apt to become stilted, mechanical, obsolete and so degenerate into empty lip service and hypocrisy. Moreover, there was just resentment at the rigor of the orthodox system, which often branded ceremonial lapses as severely as moral transgressions; set itself doggedly against the demands of the new life under the new conditions of the new world; strove to perpetuate here old world customs and observances however these might conflict with the better knowledge of the new era (as in the matter of observing a second New Year's Day when there was no longer any confusion of dates).

Then, too, Reform had been used by many as a mere license to abolish religious observances, until the Synagogue and home were like trees denuded of foliage.

The reaction was inevitable. Religious sentiments and convictions demand outward expression. Prayer is the language, ritual is the poetry of worship. The heart hunger, craving satisfaction, will not be denied. This Zangwill has set forth with dramatic power in his play, *The Next Religion*.

Our generation has come to see that Reform is not an idle whim. To reform means to alter, modify or recast a form in the religious life, so as to make it accord with the convictions and the quickened sentiments of the persons who perform the religious act. Its aim is to reveal the aesthetic and artistic beauty, to release the moral and spiritual forces enshrined in the heritage of religious treasures we possess.

This was the task to which the Conference of American Rabbis had set itself in preparing the *Union Prayerbook*. A "Book for Private Devotion" was entrusted to a committee under my leadership. By request this Kiddush service was incorporated and is now included in the new edition of Vol. I, *Union Prayerbook*. Then followed the *Union Haggadah* containing the Seder or Passover Eve service in the home. Its compilation was likewise committed to a Board of Editors under my direction. So, too, the re-adaptation of the Succoth and Hanukkah celebrations ensued and the Confirmation on Shabuot was greatly enhanced by transforming it from an old-time school exercise into a dignified and impressive religious rite.

It is a source of keen gratification to me to have had a share in all this constructive work. I am happy to be enabled now, in response to frequent requests, to republish this little book for those who desire to possess it in its attractive setting. In this era of reconstruction I am hopeful that it may be of real help to many who have come to realize that we must reconstruct before all else the home and restore to it those influences which go deepest into the making of what is permanent in the lives of our children. All the more is this imperative, now that the crushing wheels of industry have well-nigh ground into nothing the public observance of our Sabbath. Economic conditions change. Even now the Saturday half-holiday is emerging into a full holiday. The inherent force of age-long tradition has made us hold fast to the Sabbath in the face of every hostility, because in the heart of it lies the Unity of Israel. True, as Dr. E. G. Hirsh says (*Jewish Encyclopaedia*, article 'Sabbath'), "Supplementary Sunday services have been introduced in some congregations, but the facts that Sunday has an anti-Jewish implication and that in the past many allowed themselves to be martyred for the honor of the Sabbath have never failed to arouse both the indifferent and zealous."

The Sabbath has never failed to find refuge and safety within the citadel of the home. "Remember and observe" it there. While thus you enrich your own life and that of those who dwell therein, you will also best illustrate and serve the cause of Israel.

> Henry Berkowitz, rabbi,
> Congregation Rodeph Shalom
> Philadelphia, PA (1891-1924)

PREFACE TO THE THIRD EDITION

Dr. Henry Berkowitz, "The Beloved Rabbi," one of the four graduates in the first class of the Hebrew Union College in 1883, served Rodeph Shalom, actively, as its Rabbi from 1892 to 1921 (and as Rabbi Emeritus until his death in 1924). The first edition of *Sabbath Sentiment* published in 1898 was dedicated "To the Women of Israel, for they enkindle the Jewish spirit by fostering the 'Sabbath Sentiment' within their hearts and homes."

He had founded the Jewish Chautauqua Society in 1893 primarily to awaken a love and understanding of Judaism *among Jews!* He had served the Central Conference of American Rabbis as Chairman of Committees which produced the *Union Prayerbook*, the first *Union Haggadah* and other educational and devotional materials.

The second edition was published in 1921, the year of his retirement. He wrote: "It is my request that you put this little book into use in your home circle. May it exalt and deepen the ties of family devotion and so make real, in some measure, the ideals and the spiritual forces which the Congregation enshrines and which it has been the chief purpose of my ministry to emphasize."

A generation blessed by Rabbi Henry Berkowitz's spiritual leadership loved and used his *Sabbath Sentiment* in many a home. A few families to this day cherish his *Kiddush Service* and use it each Friday evening.

One such family has so loved the spirit which its continual use has engendered for all who have known the hospitality of their Sabbath table, that it makes possible this modified third edition, which is being published on the occasion of the eightieth birthday, September 24, 1966 of Leon J. Obermayer.

His family thus joyously expresses its gratitude for the love manifested in their family life, for the traditions handed on and made more beautiful by their own Sabbath observance.

May another generation of Rodeph Shalom families and their friends know a heightened joy of the Sabbath through its regular use.

> David H. Wice, rabbi,
> Congregation Rodeph Shalom,
> Philiadelphia, PA
> (1947-1981)

Marriages

Births

Deaths